Judy Hall

THE LITTLE BOOK OF
crystals
to heal mind, body, and spirit

T0299638

GODSFIELD

An Hachette UK Company
www.hachette.co.uk

First published in Great Britain in 2024
by Godsfield, an imprint of
Octopus Publishing Group Ltd
Carmelite House
50 Victoria Embankment
London EC4Y 0DZ
www.octopusbooks.co.uk

Design and layout copyright ©
Octopus Publishing Group Ltd 2024
Text copyright © Judy Hall 2018, 2024

All rights reserved. No part of this work
may be reproduced or utilized in any
form or by any means, electronic or
mechanical, including photocopying,
recording or by any information storage
and retrieval system, without the prior
written permission of the publisher.

Judy Hall asserts the moral right to be
identified as the author of this work.

Some of this material previously
appeared in *Judy Hall's Crystal
Companion*, 2018

Disclaimer: No medical claims are
made for crystals in this book and
information given is not intended
to act as a substitute for medical
treatment. Healing means bringing
mind, body and spirit back into
balance, it does not imply a cure.

ISBN 978-1-8418-1584-8

A CIP catalogue record for this book
is available from the British Library.

Printed and bound in China

10 9 8 7 6 5 4 3 2 1

Publisher: Lucy Pessell
Designer: Isobel Platt
Editor: Feyi Oyesanya
Assistant Editor: Samina Rahman
Production Manager: Pete Hunt

iStock: Box artwork: Tycson1/iStock,
jxfzsy/iStock, Wirestock/iStock
Interiors: istockphoto-1092135574 pg. 1,
Renphoto/iStock pg. 9, Miriam Doerr/
iStock pg. 14, istockphoto-1343364461
pg. 16, PamWalker68.PamWalker69/
iStock pg. 19, istockphoto-1251159526
pg. 27; **Unsplash:** Dan Farrell/Unsplash
pg. 7; **Octopus Publishing Group**
pg. 55; **Naomi Edmondson** pg. 34.

*This book contains references to "dis-ease,"
this term refers to a state that results from
physical imbalances, blocked feelings,
suppressed emotions, and negative thinking.*

FSC
www.fsc.org
MIX
Paper | Supporting
responsible forestry
FSC® C005748

Introduction 4

Crystals for the Body 28

Crystals for the Heart 50

Crystals for the Mind 64

Crystals for the Spirit 80

Introduction

It is widely known that crystals are beautiful objects, but did you know that they're also potent healing tools? With so many varieties of crystals on the market, how do you know where to start, and which crystals are right for you?

Understanding energy centres and crystal grids makes a huge difference in your interaction with your crystals, and you'll learn how to work intuitively with them to build a varied, healing toolkit that can be used and referenced in your everyday life.

This book is divided into chapters that guide you to the most suitable crystals for your needs, be they matters of the body, heart, mind or spirit. It will show you how to select, cleanse, and programme your crystals, and how to tap into their power and energy to enhance your life.

Crystals included in this kit are:
Amethyst | Citrine Quartz | Green Aventurine | Rose Quartz

You know the world
is a magical place
when Mother Earth
grows her own
jewellery.

www.wildwomansisterhood

Crystal vibrations

According to the laws of physics, everything in the universe vibrates and has its own resonant frequency. Although a term often applied to acoustics, resonant frequency relates to objects, too, as they have a mechanical or electromagnetic resonance—that is, they give off waves of energy. Where there are energetic waves, there is resonance. This resonance can be tested by specialist equipment but, for crystal workers, it is something felt rather than measured. Crystals have vibrational frequencies that range from deep and earthy ("lower") to exceedingly fine and cosmic ("higher"). These are not judgemental terms; no one vibration is better than another. Each has its part to play. Some crystals combine both ends of the spectrum, assimilating and grounding higher vibrations into the physical plane. That is to say, they step down high, refined "cosmic" vibrations so that they can be utilized in the denser vibrations of Earth. It is through these varied vibrations that crystals interact with physical and subtle bodies to bring about healing.

Earthy (lower) vibration

Earthy is the lowest and densest frequency of vibrational resonances. Earthy crystals function well in the physical world, grounding and anchoring energies. They are protective, cleansing and transmutational, soaking up negative energies and transmitting beneficial vibes.

Cosmic (high) vibration

High-vibration crystals operate at exceedingly refined resonances beyond the physicality of Earth. These cosmic crystals work at the level of spirit and soul and their effects filter "down" into the physical. Cosmic vibrations assist spiritual well-being, channelling higher consciousness to Earth, taking you into unity consciousness and universal love, accessing your soul's plane.

Healing vibration

The healing vibration covers a wide spectrum of energetic resonances. Healing means integrating mind, body and spirit, returning them to a harmonious whole. Crystals combining high vibrations with earthy resonances are effective on the physical plane, promoting well-being. Well-being is a state of mind rather than a physical condition. These crystals facilitate understanding of the effect of the mind's and soul's needs on the physical body. They dissolve underlying causes of dis-ease: spiritual, environmental, karmic, psychological, ancestral, emotional or mental imbalances accrued over many lifetimes.

Combination (lower and higher) vibrations

Combination-vibration crystals are dynamic, energetic tools for transformation and well-being. Crystals with combined earthy and high vibrations bridge frequencies of the earth-plane with cosmic dimensions to integrate dualities, infuse higher consciousness into the everyday and ensure well-being on every level. They harmonize physical and subtle-energy bodies, integrating them with the environment and multidimensions that surround us.

Colour Vibrations

Each colour has its own unique vibration. This means that different colours of a basic crystal may exhibit significant disparities in their healing effect.

- **Chalky white, grey, silver, brown or black:** Useful protectors, these crystals anchor grids. Grids are patterns laid using empowered crystals for the purpose of manifesting a desired outcome, or for cleansing and safeguarding a space. They ground the physical body and detoxify negative energies.
- **Red:** Best used for short periods, red crystals stimulate and strengthen. Activating creativity and revitalizing potency, red crystals may over-excite volatile emotions or over-energize the body, creating hyper-conditions.
- **Pink:** Ideal for long-term use, gentle pink crystals offer unconditional love, nurture and comfort, and are excellent for heart healing. They release grief, calm emotions and facilitate acceptance.

- **Orange:** Less volatile than red and appropriate for longer periods of use, orange crystals activate and release. Building up supportive energetic structures, orange attracts abundance and stimulates creativity.
- **Yellow:** Active at mental and feeling levels, yellow and golden crystals awaken and organize the mind and energize situations. They rebalance and calm emotions and overcome seasonal disorders, such as Seasonal Affective Disorder (SAD), hayfever, sensitivity to pressure changes, coughs and colds.
- **Green:** Perfect for environmental healing and the heart, green crystals calm and rebalance. They sedate energy and pacify emotions.
- **Blue:** Calming and clarifying, blue crystals facilitate communication and self-expression. They ground spiritual energy, and assist intuition and channelling.
- **Purple, indigo and lilac:** Integrating and aligning higher energies, these crystals have powerful spiritual awakening qualities, stimulating service to others. These colours cool over-heated energies.
- **White and clear:** Clarifying situations and opening intuition to gain insight, white or clear crystals purify and focus energy. They link to the highest realms of being and expanded spiritual consciousness.
- **Bi-colour:** Excellent integrators, bi-coloured crystals harmonize and unify.

What is crystal healing?

Crystal healing is an integrated, therapeutic, energetic process. It is holistic, working with the whole person rather than what is most probably a symptom of deeper dis-ease. It acts on body, psyche, soul and environment. The definition of healing that I find most useful is that illness is a dis-ease, the final manifestation of spiritual, environmental, psychological, karmic, emotional or mental imbalance or distress. Healing means bringing mind, body and spirit back into balance and facilitating evolution for the soul, it does not imply a cure.

To facilitate that "coming back into balance" I use crystals. Why so many? Well, each crystal offers unique properties. There may be a need to cleanse, unblock, sedate or activate energies. For that, different colours and disparate crystals are required, according to the vibrational state of the person or environment. There is no "one size fits all" in crystal work. Each person has their own specific frequency, which differs from anyone else's, due to past experiences, ancestral inheritance, environment, nutrition, beliefs and so on. Finding the crystal that resonates with you and brings you back into balance is key to maintaining well-being and evolving spiritually.

Crystal affinities

Across aeons of time, the perceived properties of crystals have remained remarkably consistent. Hematite has an affinity with blood, exactly as it did in Mesopotamia and Egypt thousands of years ago. Selenite is still regarded as crystallized divine light. A vast body of knowledge has built up regarding affinities between crystals and organs of the body and chakras, mapping physiological interaction. Crystals energetically regulate the hormonal and other systems in addition to bringing mind, body and spirit into harmony. Light and colour have a profound effect on the functioning of pineal, pituitary and other glands in the body, supporting traditional use.

Crystals for healing

The most direct method of using a crystal for healing is to place it over the site of dis-ease or pain and leave it in place for 5–15 minutes once or twice a day. You could, of course, wear a crystal for long periods of time, but remember to cleanse it regularly. The other main methods are through chakras or grids. The crystal activates, cleanses and re-energizes the energy centre and organs connected with it, realigning and harmonizing chakras where appropriate, or purifies and protects the whole body or space.

A HEALING CHALLENGE

If you find yourself having a strong reaction or feeling particularly averse to a specific colour or crystal, it may have an incompatible vibration. Or it could indicate something you are hiding from yourself. This may be a feeling or an attitude repressed because you, unconsciously, deem it "unacceptable" or too painful. Such repression leads to psychosomatic dis-ease (caused by internal conflict or stress). The suppressed feeling manifests itself physically within the body, or as a subtle sense of all not being well. This feeling is sometimes projected into the outside world. It could be that the crystal is having a cathartic or detoxifying effect, or triggering internal conflicts and conflicting agendas in your unconscious mind. Putting the crystal aside and gently exploring the cause of your reaction with a cleansing and grounding crystal such as Smoky Quartz at your feet assists. Once you have drawn off the initial source of distress, and dispersed it into the grounding crystal, you may need the support of a crystal that instils a complementary healing resonance. So, if the crystal has triggered jealousy and resentment, for instance, holding Rose Quartz would dispel this.

Crystal selection, care and programming

The easiest way to select your crystal is to use your intuition. Glance through relevant crystal portraits in this book. When a particular crystal catches your eye, focus on it. The same applies when you purchase a crystal. Choose one that catches your attention. Or, if you are unused to trusting your intuition, dowse for the right crystal. Finger-dowsing provides an easy way to select stones.

To ensure that a crystal works to its highest potential, attune it to your personal vibration, asking it to work for your highest good.

To finger-dowse

Loop the thumb and finger of your non-dominant hand
together. Slip your other thumb and finger through the
loop and close together. Ask your question. Pull steadily.
If the loop breaks, the answer is "no." If the loop holds, the
answer is "yes."

To pendulum-dowse

Hold your pendulum between thumb and forefinger of
your most receptive hand with about a hand's length of
chain hanging down. Wrap the remaining chain around
your fingers. Hold the pendulum over the crystal or its
photograph in this book. To ascertain a "yes" and "no"
response: Hold the pendulum over your knee and ask:
"Is my name [state correct name]?" The direction that
the pendulum swings indicates "yes." Ask: "Is my name
[incorrect name]?" to establish "no."

The pendulum may swing in one direction for "yes"
and at right angles to that axis for "no," or a backward and
forward swing for "no" and a circular motion for "yes."
A wobble indicates "maybe," that it is not appropriate at
that time or the wrong question is being asked. If so, check
you are framing the question correctly. If the pendulum
stops, it is inappropriate to ask at that time.

Crystal cleansing methods

Crystals soak up vibrations—negative and positive—by absorbing energy from the environment. Unless cleansed, a crystal carries energy from everyone who has handled it or places where it spent time. Crystals require frequent cleansing and re-energizing.

- **Water:** Robust, non-soluble crystals are cleansed by running under water for a few moments and placing in sun or moonlight to recharge.
- **Brown rice:** Place crystal in brown rice overnight and recharge afterwards in sunlight. Do not reuse the rice—compost or dispose of it.
- **Return to earth:** Robust crystals may be buried. Mark the spot. After retrieving the crystal, leave it in sunlight to recharge.

- **Smudge:** Smoke from a smudge stick or incense cleanses a crystal before recharging in sunlight.
- **Crystal:** A large Quartz, Citrine, Chlorite Quartz or Carnelian cleanses and recharges a smaller crystal but needs cleansing afterwards. (Although Citrine and Kyanite are self-cleansing, they still benefit from regular cleansing.) Placing a small crystal on a larger version of itself recharges a crystal, restoring its energetic frequency.
- **Light:** Passing a crystal through light from a candle or visualizing it surrounded by light purifies it. Placing the crystal in sun or moonlight recharges it.

Activating your crystal

A crystal needs to be activated and programmed to begin working. Rub your hands briskly together to activate your palm chakras. Hold the crystal in your hands and wait a few moments to attune to it. Check out how you feel. A crystal in harmony with your energy field feels peaceful and calm, or buzzing and busy. If a crystal feels unpleasant, it may have triggered a release or may not be appropriate.

Picture light surrounding the crystal and formulate your intention. Be specific because focused intention is part of the process, but don't limit your intention. If using the crystal for healing, say precisely for which condition and the result you seek. But leave room for underlying factors to materialize.

Always add the statement: "This or something more for the highest good." This opens the way for things to happen that you may not have envisaged.

When you are totally in tune, say out loud:

"I programme [ask] this crystal for/to [state your purpose]. This or something greater for the highest good of all who come in contact with it."

Wear the crystal, place it on your body, position it where you see it frequently or keep it in your pocket.

Maintaining your crystals

Treat your crystals gently. Keep coloured crystals out of sunlight as they may fade. Layered or clustered stones such as Halite are water-soluble, eroding in a damp atmosphere. Polished surfaces are easily scratched, but tumbled stones are more robust. When not in use, wrap your crystals in a silk or velvet scarf. This protects the crystal against absorbing negative emanations. It avoids a mishmash of crystal energies permeating your home or environment and allows space for those that are working to function optimally.

Crystal grids and layouts

Crystal grids are energy transmitters laid out according to the principles of sacred geometry. Ranging from the simplest of shapes to the most complex forms, they harness fundamental forces of the universe, synergizing them with crystal vibrations into a vast energetic net. These work at personal and environmental levels.

Layouts are particularly useful for protecting your space and transmuting detrimental energies They fill the space with beneficial energy.

Cleanse crystals before laying in a grid. A few basic grids are all you need, and for additional crystal ideas, see the crystal portraits.

TRIANGLE

A triangular grid cleanses and protects a space. Triangulation neutralizes negative energy and EMFs (electromotive forces), and draws in positive vibes. This layout is particularly helpful placed around your bed.

- Place one crystal midway along a wall or above the head.
- Place a crystal in each opposite corner or below either side of the feet.
- Join points with a crystal wand or the power of your mind.

FIVE-POINTED STAR

The five-pointed star is a useful protection layout or caller-in of cosmic energies and healing.

- Place one crystal at the top point.
- Follow the line down to the bottom right of the star.
- Follow the line up to the top left.
- Follow the line straight across.
- Follow the line down to the bottom left.
- Join up the star with a wand, returning to the first crystal to complete the circuit.
- You can place a keystone in the centre.

STAR OF DAVID

The Star of David is a traditional protection layout that creates a perfect manifestation space.

- Lay the first triangle and join up the points. (Lay it facing downwards to contain energy and facing up to draw it in.)
- Lay a second triangle over the top but facing in the opposite direction and join up the points.
- A keystone can be placed in the centre or an anchor stone below the grid.

SPIRAL

Spirals are abundance creators and re-energizing layouts. A spiral draws energy into the centre or radiates it out as required.

- If drawing energy into the centre, start at the outer edge. If radiating energy out, start at the inner point.
- A keystone can be placed at the centre.
- Lay crystals in a spiral. (If using crystals with points, position point towards the centre to bring energy in and point outwards to radiate it into the environment.)

Crystal families

In this section you'll find the characteristics and generic properties of major healing crystal groups.

Generator
Quartz pillar

Orange River
Quartz

Lithium Quartz

Ajoite

QUARTZ

- Master healer and paterfamilias of the largest crystal family on the planet.
- Quartz generates, stores and radiates vibrant energy.
- Quartz purifies and amplifies energy, working in harmony with each individual using it. It doubles the biomagnetic field around the body and takes energy back to the most perfect state possible. It is a master healer, so you can use it for any condition, although different colours and forms work better for specific tasks, according to their vibration.
- A crystal computer, Quartz is ideal for programming for distance healing, communication or manifestation, as its stable energy holds the programme for long periods and radiates the energy appropriately.

AGATE

Blue Lace Agate

- Stabilizing; perfect for grounding energy.
- It acts slowly but surely. This centring stone provides an unshakeable sense of safety and security. Soothing and calming, it brings balance at the physical, emotional and intellectual levels, harmonizing yin and yang, positive and negative.

Moss Agate

- Agate has a powerful cleansing effect, physically and emotionally. Gently dissolving anger and resentment, it heals emotional trauma that underlies an inability to accept love.

JASPER

Kambaba Jasper

Red Jasper

- Supreme nurturer.
- Jasper is extremely stable and protective, grounding all areas of life. A reliable support during prolonged illness or traumatic events, it prevents burn-out.
- Jasper facilitates ending situations that are no longer for your highest good with gentleness and grace, and protects your energies during tie-cutting. This nurturing stone facilitates shamanic journeys, dowsing and dream recall, providing protection. Jasper absorbs negative energy, balances yin and yang, and aligns the physical, emotional and mental bodies with the etheric realm.

CALCITE

Blue Calcite

Moldavite
Calcite

- Purifying.
- Although working slowly and gently, Calcite speeds up development and growth.
- Calcite removes stagnant energies, revitalizing the body and the environment. It encourages calcium uptake in bones, but dissolves calcifications, strengthening the skeleton and joints.
- The crystal promotes inner peace and spiritual connection. It promotes emotional intelligence, opening the heart to restore hope and inner serenity. It increases trust in yourself and others.

GARNET

Red Garnet

Uvarovite
Garnet

- Revitalizer.
- Garnet is an energizing crystal of regeneration and rejuvenation. It boosts the energy of an entire system and stabilizes it.
- Garnet has a long history of inspiring love, devotion and commitment.
- Useful in a crisis, this stone instils courage into seemingly hopeless situations, especially when life has fragmented or is traumatic. The crystal also fosters mutual assistance.
- Garnet sharpens perceptions, dissolves ingrained, outdated behaviour patterns and bestows self-confidence.

OPAL

Blue Opal

Black Opal

- Protective Opal reaches out to cosmic consciousness and induces metaphysical and mystical visions.
- Opals are strong-acting and virtually instant in their effect.
- A karmic stone, Opal teaches that what you put out comes back. It amplifies deeply ingrained traits, whether those traits are deemed "good" or "bad," and draws characteristics to the surface for transformation and to discover the gifts hidden within.

TOURMALINE

Paraiba Tourmaline

Blue and Black Tourmaline

- Psychic shield.
- Tourmaline cleanses, purifies and transforms toxic energy into a lighter vibration.
- Tourmaline facilitates understanding yourself and others. It takes you deep into your self, promoting self-confidence, diminishing fear and banishing victim mentality. The stone promotes inspiration, compassion, tolerance and prosperity.
- It balances the right and left hemispheres of the brain and transmutes negative thought patterns into positive ones. It improves hand-to-eye coordination, and the assimilation and translation of coded information.

Hints and tips

- Choose stones appropriate for your personal energy field.
- Crystals do not have to be perfect. Chipped, raw or oddly shaped crystals work equally well.
- Cleanse and reactivate your crystals regularly.
- Take your time. Switch off your phone.
- Explore crystals without preconceptions or expectations.
- Remember that changes may occur over time rather than immediately.
- Be prepared for a healing challenge, dizziness or nausea to occur. If so, remove crystal(s) and sit with a grounding crystal such as Smoky Quartz or Flint at your feet or on your belly. Breathe deeply and slowly, making the out-breath longer than the in-breath. Push the energies down through your feet until equilibrium returns.
- Drink plenty of pure spring water after a crystal session.
- Rest and relax after a session to allow the energies to integrate.

Crystals
for the body

Crystals in this section have been specially chosen for
their healing effect on the physical and subtle-energy
bodies. As we have noted, illness is a dis-ease, the final
manifestation of spiritual, environmental, psychological,
karmic, emotional or mental imbalance or distress.
Healing through the chakras is an important part of
crystal healing, as each chakra is traditionally linked
to organs and physiological processes within the body.
Crystal layouts over a chakra or along the whole system
return the body to balance. However, crystals can be laid
over an organ or gridded around the body to support
well-being.

COMMON CAUSES OF
PHYSICAL DIS-EASE

- Malfunctioning immune system
- Viral, bacterial, environmental or chemical pathogens, including the side effects of previous medication or treatment
- Physical injury
- Stress and tension or inadequate rest
- Toxic emotions or negative thoughts
- Emotional exhaustion and energy drain
- Shock or trauma
- Anxiety or fear
- EMF pollution and geopathic stress, sick building syndrome and the like
- Karmic or transgenerational transfer and Ancestral Healing
- Soulplan, which maps out the soul's intention for the present lifetime

Common causes of dis-ease

Crystals are an holistic healing system that treats causes rather than relieving symptoms. Dis-ease is a state of imbalance. It eventually results in physical or psychosomatic ailments. Psychosomatic does not mean imaginary. Internal conflict or stress, toxic emotions and destructive thought patterns directly affect the body's ability to function optimally. Except in cases of direct physical injury, dis-ease establishes itself at an energetic level first. It is located in chakras and subtle-energy bodies. If not restored to equilibrium, dis-ease moves into the physical body to create deeper maladies.

Intervention with crystals restores energetic balance before dis-ease establishes a permanent hold. Even in cases of physical injury, crystals such as Magnetite and Bloodstone have a long history of assisting in the relief of inflammation, bruising, broken bones and muscular aches and pains. The minerals in crystals are still part of medicine today. Lithium-rich crystals such as Kunzite form the base of anti-anxiety medication, and Klinopotilolith creates a powerful chemotherapy drug.

EXERCISE

SUPPORTING THE
IMMUNE SYSTEM

Keeping the immune system energetically supported
ensures well-being. If the immune system is running too
slowly, invigorating healing crystals, such as Bloodstone
or Cherry Quartz taped over the higher heart chakra
(mid upper chest) or gently tapped either side of
the breastbone stimulates it. If it is running too fast,
soothing crystals such as Que Sera, Emerald Quartz or
Quantum Quattro calm it.

- Lie down and place the immune crystal in the centre
  of the upper chest midway along the breastbone.
- Relax and breathe gently.
- Leave in place for 15–20 minutes before removing.
- Cleanse crystal after use.

EXERCISE

ALL-PURPOSE REVITALIZER LAYOUT

Suitable crystals: Red Jasper, Hematite Quartz, Flint keystone

- Lie down and place a crystal either side of the base of your armpits.
- Place a crystal on your pubic bone.
- Join up the triangle with the power of your mind.
- Lay two crystals either side of your waist.
- Lay a crystal in the centre of your breastbone.
- Join up the second triangle with the power of your mind.
- Place a keystone on the navel.
- Keep in place for 15–20 minutes.
- Remove stones in the reverse order—that is, keystone first.
- Cleanse crystals after use.

Chakras, physiology and dis-ease

Laying crystals on the chakras or auric field corrects imbalances and systems of the body. The chakras and how well they are operating play a vital role in regulating dis-ease. Chakras may be over-active and need calming, or under-active and blocked, in which case they need stimulating, which is why traditional chakra colour correspondences may not be appropriate. Many crystals relate to specific chakras but are not the "traditional" colour, because this colour system was only formulated just over 100 years ago, whereas the chakra-related crystals have been in use for issues connected to those chakras for hundreds, if not thousands, of years. A crystal from the other side of the colour wheel may be more suitable.

CHAKRAS AND PHYSIOLOGY

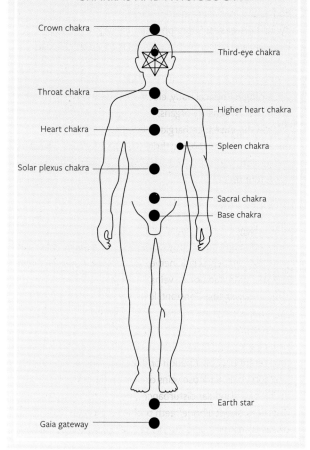

Crown chakra

Third-eye chakra

Throat chakra

Higher heart chakra

Heart chakra

Spleen chakra

Solar plexus chakra

Sacral chakra

Base chakra

Earth star

Gaia gateway

GAIA GATEWAY

- **Physiology:** Subtle-energy bodies, linking into Earth's subtle bodies and meridian system.
- **Typical dis-eases:** Supra-physical. Inability to ground kundalini and higher frequencies leads to subtle dis-ease.

EARTH STAR

- **Physiology:** Physical body, electrical and meridian systems, sciatic nerve, sensory organs.
- **Typical dis-eases:** Lethargic or invasive. Myalgic encephalomyelitis (ME), arthritis, cancer, muscular disorders, depression, psychiatric disturbances, auto-immune diseases, persistent tiredness.

BASE

- **Physiology:** "Fight or flight" response, adrenals, bladder, elimination and immune systems, gonads, kidneys, lower back, lower extremities, sciatic nerve, lymph system, prostate gland, rectum, teeth and bones, veins.
- **Typical dis-eases:** Constant, low-level or flare-up. Adrenal response is permanently activated. Stiffness or tingling in joints, poor circulation in lower limbs, sciatica, chronic lower back pain, renal, reproductive or rectal disorders, fluid retention, constipation or diarrhea, prostate problems, haemorrhoids, varicose veins or hernias, bipolar disorder, addictions, glandular disturbances, personality and anxiety disorders, skeletal/bone/teeth problems, auto-immune diseases, insomnia and disturbed sleep, waking unrefreshed.

SACRAL

- **Physiology:** Bladder and gallbladder, immune and elimination systems, kidneys, large and small intestine, lumbar and pelvic region, sacrum, spleen, ovaries, testes, uterus.
- **Typical dis-eases:** Pernicious and psychosomatic. Premenstrual syndrome (PMS), muscle cramps, sciatica, reproductive blockages or diseases, prostate problems, impotence, infertility, fibroids, endometriosis, allergies, addictions, eating disorders, diabetes, liver or intestinal dysfunction, irritable bowel syndrome, chronic back pain, urinary infections.

SOLAR PLEXUS

- **Physiology:** Adrenals, digestive system, liver, lymphatic system, metabolism, muscles, pancreas, skin, small intestine, stomach, eyesight.
- **Typical dis-eases:** Emotional and demanding. Stomach ulcers, ME, adrenaline imbalances, SAD, insomnia and chronic anxiety, digestive problems, malabsorption of nutrients, gallstones, pancreatic failure, liver problems, eczema and skin conditions, eating disorders, phobias, multiple sclerosis.

SPLEEN

- **Physiology:** Spleen, pancreas, lymphatic system and liver.
- **Typical dis-eases:** Depletion and lack. Lethargy, anaemia, low blood sugar, diabetes, pancreatitis, liver problems, auto-immune diseases.

HEART

- **Physiology:** Chest, circulation, heart, lungs, shoulders, thymus, respiratory system.
- **Typical dis-eases:** Psychosomatic and reactive. Heart attacks, angina, chest infections, asthma, frozen shoulder, ulcers, persistent cough, wheeziness, pneumonia, high cholesterol, mastitis, breast cysts, pancreatic problems.

HIGHER HEART (THYMUS)

- **Physiology:** Psychic and physical immune systems, thymus gland, lymphatic system, elimination and purification organs.
- **Typical dis-eases:** Disordered immune system. Auto-immune diseases, repeated viral and bacterial infections, coughs, colds, glandular fever, ME, multiple sclerosis (MS), HIV/AIDS, arteriosclerosis, flushing of chest and neck, tinnitus, vitiligo, psoriasis, alopecia, thyroid problems.

THROAT

- **Physiology:** Ears, nose, respiratory and nervous system, sinuses, skin, throat, thyroid, parathyroid, tongue, tonsils, speech and body language, metabolism.
- **Typical dis-eases:** Block communication. Sore throat/quinsy, lump in throat, difficulty in swallowing, inflammation of trachea, sinus, constant colds and viral infections, tinnitus, ear infections, jaw pain, gum disease, tooth problems, thyroid imbalances, high blood pressure, irritable bowel, psychosomatic and metabolic dis-eases.

THIRD EYE (BROW)

- **Physiology:** Brain, ears, eyes, neurological and endocrine systems, pineal and pituitary glands, hypothalamus, production of serotonin and melatonin, temperature control, scalp, sinuses.
- **Typical dis-eases:** Metaphysical. Migraine, mental overwhelm, schizophrenia, cataracts, iritis, spinal and neurological disorders, sinus and ear infections, high blood pressure, memory loss, eye problems. Nervous or hormonal disorders, hot or cold flashes, excessive perspiration, skin conditions such as psoriasis, eczema, impetigo, hives; allergies, sinus problems, adenoid and ear disorders, lack of energy and/or sex drive.

CROWN

- **Physiology:** Brain, central nervous system, hair, hypothalamus, pituitary gland, spine, subtle-energy bodies, cerebellum, nervous and motor control, posture and balance.
- **Typical dis-eases:** Disconnection and isolation. Metabolic syndrome, hypertension, vague "unwellness," lethargy, nervous system disturbances, electromagnetic and environmental sensitivity, depression, dementia, ME, Parkinson's disease, insomnia or excessive sleepiness, "biological clock" disturbances, SAD, impaired coordination, headaches, migraine, anxiety, insomnia, depression, multiple personality disorder, mental breakdown.

BLOODSTONE
(HELIOTROPE)
Immune stimulator

Bloodstone is the go-to stone of choice for physical ailments, especially when placed over the higher heart (thymus) chakra. An excellent blood cleanser, it regulates blood-flow and assists circulation. Use at onset of acute infections. Bloodstone stimulates the flow of lymph and metabolic processes, revitalizes and re-energizes the body and detoxifies liver, intestines, kidneys, spleen and bladder. It reduces irritability, aggressiveness and impatience.

Bloodstone is an excellent grounding shield, offering protection against pathogens as well as deflecting bullying or threatening situations.

Vibration: Earthy
Chakra: Higher heart; aligns all
Physiology: Immune system, blood, blood-rich organs, liver, intestines, kidneys, spleen and bladder
Cleansing: All

SMOKY QUARTZ
Detoxification

One of the most effective grounding and clearing crystals, relaxing Smoky Quartz improves the tolerance of stress. This stone provides pain relief. A layout of slow-release Smoky Quartz pointing out from the body prevents a healing crisis. It assists with assimilation of minerals, fluid regulation and detoxification of the body or environment, including EMFs. The crystal heals toxic emotional conditions, overcoming fear and lack of trust, instilling a sense of safety and protection. In psychic work, Smoky Quartz facilitates connection to the lower shamanic worlds and the astral plane, shielding against psychic attack and transmuting negative energies. It raises personal vibrations during meditation.

Vibration: Earthy and high
Chakra: Gaia gateway, earth star, base; aligns all
Physiology: Quartz maintains all organs and systems in the body
Cleansing: All

POPPY JASPER
Passion reviver

Passionate and potent, Poppy Jasper is gentle and fiery. It activates the base chakra to bring vitality and joy, grounding energy into the body and stimulating libido. Conversely, it calms an over-active base chakra and disperses sexual frustration, soothing an over-stimulated sex-drive. Poppy Jasper balances yin and yang, aligning physical, emotional and mental bodies with the etheric realm. Clearing electromagnetic and environmental pollution, it sustains during stress or prolonged illness, inducing tranquillity and wholeness. Calming emotions, this stone imparts determination, courage and motivation. Poppy Jasper extends sexual pleasure. Re-energizing the body, it also assists birth and rebirthing.

Vibration: Earthy to high
Chakra: Base, sacral; energizes all
Physiology: Circulatory, digestive and sexual organs
Cleansing: All

CARNELIAN
Creativity

Rejuvenating Carnelian is a powerful motivator with great vitality. Perfect for the base and sacral chakras, it re-energizes the whole energetic system. Paradoxically, it soothes inflammation and over-active conditions, calming where appropriate. Carnelian supports positive life choices, turning dreams into reality. It reverses mental lethargy and transmutes anger or victimhood into empowerment and motivation to get things moving. Stabilizing, Carnelian anchors into the present reality. Removing extraneous thoughts in meditation, it helps you to be fully present. Carnelian cleanses and re-energizes other stones.

Vibration: Earthy
Chakra: Base, sacral
Physiology: Metabolism, blood and blood-rich organs, liver, spleen, reproductive system, lower back, kidneys, bones, ligaments
Cleansing: All

YELLOW JASPER
Companionship

Yellow Jasper infuses body, mind and soul with hope. A stone of the sun, it overcomes depression and anxiety. A useful emotional support for psychosomatic conditions, it assists your earthly journey and keeps you on your soulpath. Yellow Jasper sustains during stressful times and chronic illness. This stone protects and clears the body of environmental toxins and impurities, and emotional angst or outgrown patterns. It cleanses and detoxifies internal organs, including liver, gallbladder and intestines. Yellow Jasper creates a shield, returning gossip and negativity to its source. It overcomes dyspraxia, or accident proneness.

Vibration: Earthy
Chakra: Sacral, solar plexus
Physiology: Circulatory, digestive and sexual organs
Cleansing: All

MOOKAITE JASPER
Versatility

Creating a balance between inner and outer experiences, Mookaite Jasper protects and takes you into a calm centre to wait out any storm. It helps face up to the aging process, appreciating the wisdom of age rather than the drawbacks. Mookaite acts as a companion for the bereaved or lonely, and contacts souls on other planes. It encourages versatility, pointing out all possibilities and assisting in choosing the appropriate one, but encourages facing present circumstances calmly if change is not possible. It is physically stabilizing: mainly red, fortifying the immune system, and yellow, calming it.

Vibration: Earthy
Chakra: Earth star, base, sacral
Physiology: Circulatory, digestive and sexual organs
Cleansing: All

JADE
Purity

Serene Jade is cleansing, assisting the body's filtration and elimination organs and facilitating toxic emotional and pernicious core-belief release. Stabilizing the personality, it promotes self-sufficiency, releasing negative thoughts and soothing the mind. Jade stimulates creative ideas, making tasks appear less complex so that they are acted upon immediately. This protective stone keeps the wearer from harm and creates harmony. Integrating mind and body, it releases limiting beliefs, opening the mind to new possibilities. The stone has long been associated with attracting prosperity and good health. It traditionally maintains kidney function. Each colour has additional properties.

Vibration: High
Chakra: All, according to colour
Physiology: Kidneys, suprarenal glands, cellular and skeletal systems
Cleansing: All

BLUE LACE AGATE
Ultimate communication

The perfect communication stone, Blue Lace Agate frees up the throat chakra, allowing expression of thoughts and emotions. It clears speech impediments and counteracts feelings of being judged, encouraging a new mode of expression. Feelings that have previously been repressed are calmly given voice. It helps men accept their sensitive, feeling nature. Blue Lace Agate facilitates the expression of spiritual truth. The stone calms stress, neutralizing anger or frustration. It soothes inflammation and fever, releases shoulder and neck problems, and overcomes thyroid deficiencies and throat or lymph infections. Directing vibrations appropriately, Blue Lace Agate enhances sound healing.

Vibration: Medium
Chakra: Throat, third eye, heart, crown
Physiology: Throat, thyroid
Cleansing: All

GRAPE CHALCEDONY
(GRAPE AGATE)
Grace

Sedative and calming, Grape Chalcedony cleanses perception, identifying what is important, helping you sit in stillness and simply be. Activating the karma of grace that says you only have to do enough, its tranquil gentleness dismantles defences and opens your heart. A wonderful emotional support, soothing fears, it heals the inner darkness that sneakily whispers fear into the heart. Drawing like-minded people together for mutual support, it reminds you that, even when you appear to be totally alone, help is available. A stone of inspiration that encourages trust, Grape Chalcedony facilitates finding your karmic strengths. It decongests the body through lymph flow.

Vibration: High
Chakra: All, especially solar plexus and higher
Physiology: Stomach, brain and brain chemistry, lymphatic and nervous systems, ameliorates panic attacks, bipolar disorder or anxiety
Cleansing: Avoid water

MOONSTONE
Intuition

Moonstone enhances intuition and psychic abilities. It calms emotions, reducing instability, and prevents overreactions to situations and emotional triggers. It clears outdated emotional patterning and is the perfect antidote to calm excessively aggressive people. Moonstone soothes stress at any level. A powerful healer for the female reproductive cycle and menstrual-related dis-ease, it assists birth. Water-attuned, it stabilizes fluid imbalances and resets the biorhythmic clock. Helpful for shock, insomnia and sleep-walking, it calms hyperactive children. Wear in accordance with phases of the moon.

Vibration: High to extremely high, according to type
Chakra: Third eye, solar plexus
Physiology: Digestive and reproductive systems, female reproductive cycle, menstrual-related dis-ease, pineal gland, hormonal balance, fluid imbalances, biorhythmic clock, skin, hair, eyes
Cleansing: Avoid water

QUE SERA
(LLANOITE, VULCANITE)
Synergistic healing

A powerful combination containing Quartz, Feldspar, Calcite, Kaolinite, Hematite, Magnetite, Leucozone and Clinozoisite, Que Sera facilitates standing in your own power, released from self-imposed obligations. If you take the troubles of the world on your shoulders and cannot say no, and especially if you dwell on problems, Que Sera finds constructive solutions. A potent healer, Que Sera assists all organs and systems of the physical body. Place it wherever dis-ease or depletion exists.

Vibration: High
Chakra: Earth star, base, sacral
Physiology: Immune system. *See* Quartz, page 22
Cleansing: All

Crystals
for the heart

The heart governs the psyche, consciously or unconsciously, directing the body's reactions to social and physical environments. The heart has emotional intelligence. It deals with gut reactions and intuitions, unconditional love and compassion—and motivation. It encompasses not only relationships but also emotions, attitudes and feelings—and the internal conflicts and multiple agendas arising from past lives and interlife agreements. If noxious emotions and heartbreak are stuck in the emotional body or heart chakra, it leads to psychosomatic dis-ease and challenging relationships. Crystals gently release toxic emotions, instilling a more appropriate feeling.

Emotions and psyche

From the viewpoint of crystal healing, many dis-eases have an emotional basis, being caused not by injury but instead by underlying factors such as stress, emotional repression over a long period, toxic memories, shame, disappointment or spiritual discomfort. Even those that are apparently caused by pathogens may reveal an underlying psychic susceptibility.

"Illness has a purpose; it has to resolve the conflict, to repress it, or to prevent what is already repressed from entering consciousness," wrote Georg W. Groddeck (19th-century Swiss physician).

In Chinese medicine, for instance, grief is associated with the lungs. If grief is not fully expressed and let go, or is held onto from other lives, then the lungs cannot function optimally. Similarly, anger or resentment affects the liver and fear affects the kidneys, both filtration systems for clearing toxicity from the body. Previous life attitudes such as hard-heartedness or experiences such as heartbreak play out in the present life as "a heart condition." Healing the heart and emotional body releases the underlying condition.

COMMON CAUSES OF
EMOTIONAL DIS-EASE

- Past experiences: trauma from present or previous lives, shame and distress, personal or familial, lodges itself in the emotional body or heart chakra.
- Defence mechanism: "un-wellness" avoids confrontation with the challenges of life or dealing with inner emotional problems. Clearing the chakras, especially the base and earth star, resolves this.
- Powerlessness: being unable to take control of life and an inability to extend compassion to yourself due to a blocked heart chakra leads to psychosomatic dis-ease.
- Holding onto the past: living in the past, or bringing conditions forward, personal or familial, creates emotional dis-ease and is held in the karmic and ancestral bodies and past-life or causal vortex chakras, as well as the heart.

HEART HEALING

Anger, resentment, jealousy, guilt, shame and the like are self-destructive emotions. Feelings may be held onto consciously or unconsciously, repressed deep in the psyche until they turn on the body or mind through the physical and psychic immune system. Placing a crystal on relevant chakras, or gridding them around the body, gently releases this emotional dross, and positive feelings such as self-worth and confidence take their place.

A simple Star of David grid heals the heart and clears heartbreak, jealousy and so on. It can be placed over the actual heart or positioned close to a bed or where it will be seen often.
Suitable crystals: Clearing — Smoky Quartz, Peridot and Rhodonite. Love-infusing — Rose Quartz, Garnet and Rhodochrosite.

- Lay a downward-facing triangle with appropriate clearing crystals and join up.
- Lay an upward-facing triangle with love-infusing crystals and join up.

BLACK OBSIDIAN
Deep soul-cleanser

A deep healer, Obsidian offers insight into causes of dis-ease. It removes blockages and debris from past lives and reverses previous misuse of power, addressing power issues on all levels. The stone blocks psychic attack and removes negative spiritual influences. It anchors the spirit into the body. Obsidian brings deep-seated emotions and issues to the surface, accessing your shadow and integrating positive qualities hidden there. It works extremely fast, but you may need other crystals to deal with issues arising from it. The stone clarifies the mind and clears confusion. It assists the body's structures to energetically detoxify, blocking geopathic stress and environmental pollution.

Vibration: Earthy
Chakra: Earth star, base, sacral
Physiology: Digestion, detoxification, arteries, joints, circulation, prostate
Cleansing: All

ROSE QUARTZ
Unconditional love

Compassionate Rose Quartz carries unconditional love and acceptance, bringing deep emotional healing and promoting the self-love that is essential before love is accepted from others. The stone teaches that unconditional love does not mean sacrificing yourself, being walked on or abused.

A powerful stone for healing grief and loss, Rose Quartz strengthens empathy and sensitivity, enhancing all interactions with others. It encourages self-forgiveness and absolution for those who have, apparently, wronged you, revealing their role in your soulplan. The beautiful stone invokes self-trust and enhances self-worth.

Vibration: Extremely high
Chakra: Heart, higher heart
Physiology: Adrenals
Cleansing: All

RHODOCHROSITE
Selfless love

Rhodochrosite encourages the spontaneous expression of feelings, including passionate and erotic urges. Removing denial, it teaches the heart to assimilate painful feelings without shutting down. Identifying ongoing relationship patterns, it reveals the purpose behind an experience. It is the stone par excellence for healing sexual abuse, and is wonderful for people who feel unloved. A powerful heart healer, it brings lightness into life. This compassionate stone lifts a depressed mood and imparts a dynamic attitude to life. It integrates spiritual with material energies. Rhodochrosite attracts a soulmate, but this may not be a blissful experience as soulmates assist with all forms of karmic lessons, even harsh ones.

Vibration: Earthy and high
Chakra: Solar plexus, heart
Physiology: Reproductive, respiratory and circulatory systems, kidneys, eyes, blood pressure, heartbeat, thyroid
Cleansing: All

PINK OPAL
Emotional healing

The gentle, yet high frequency of Pink Opal heals the emotional body and repairs its connection to the three-chambered heart chakra. An effective heart-healer, Pink Opal disperses wounds and anxiety and gently dissolves painful memories blocking the heart. This tranquil Opal suits highly sensitive people who need to approach crystal work slowly, letting go of long-suppressed pain. It heals issues carried forward from past lives, replacing them with compassion for your Self. Dissipating stress, this is excellent for anyone who has lost the sweetness in life. It can help balance blood-sugar levels.

Vibration: Medium high
Chakra: Heart, higher heart, spleen
Physiology: Pancreas
Cleansing: Avoid water

RHODONITE
Trauma-soother

Rhodonite soothes the nervous system. An excellent first-aid remedy for trauma or shock, it is an effective wound-healer. It calms and supports mind, body and soul in challenging situations. Revealing all sides of an issue, it is beneficial in cases of emotional self-destruction or physical self-harming, codependency or abuse, healing the heart trauma that results. Rhodonite dissolves memories of abuse and emotional scars gathered over many lifetimes, replacing them with love and forgiveness. It also helps you to achieve your highest potential. It builds confidence and opens the heart to unconditional love. The stone assists lovers reach tantric union.

Vibration: High
Chakra: Solar plexus, heart, higher heart
Physiology: Nervous system, lungs, ears, bones, joints
Cleansing: All

PERIDOT
Cleansing power

Peridot teaches that holding onto people, or the past, is counter-productive. A powerful cleanser, Peridot neutralizes toxins on all levels, alleviating jealousy, resentment, spitefulness and anger. It enhances confidence and self-assertion without aggression. Peridot purifies the subtle and physical bodies and mind, releasing "old baggage." Looking back to the past to find the gift in your experiences, it shows how to forgive yourself and move on. Mistakes are acknowledged and learned from. Past-their-sell-by-date contracts, promises, burdens, guilt or obsessions are cleared, so that a new frequency is accessed. This visionary crystal helps you to understand your spiritual purpose.

Vibration: Medium to high
Chakra: Heart, solar plexus
Physiology: Soft tissues, metabolism, skin, heart, thymus, lungs, gallbladder, spleen, intestinal tract, eyes
Cleansing: Avoid water

EMERALD
Successful love

Emerald brings domestic bliss and loyalty, enhancing unity and unconditional love. The stone keeps a partnership in balance. Colour change is said to signal unfaithfulness. Opening the heart chakra, it calms emotions. This life-affirming stone has great integrity. It ensures physical, emotional and mental equilibrium, eliminating negativity. Emerald gives the strength of character to overcome the misfortunes of life and inspires deep inner knowing, broadening vision. A wisdom stone, promoting discernment, truth and eloquent expression, it brings to the surface what is unconsciously known. Emerald is beneficial to mutual understanding within a group, stimulating cooperation.

Vibration: High
Chakra: Heart, higher heart
Physiology: Sinuses, lungs, heart, spine, muscles, eyes, liver, pancreas
Cleansing: All

MALACHITE
Ultimate detoxification

Breaking outworn patterns and unwanted ties especially
with energy vampires or previous partners, Malachite
releases toxic emotions and inhibitions, encouraging
free expression of feelings. It may induce a catharsis
and require additional stones, such as Smoky Quartz, to
calm the abreaction (the release of a previously repressed
emotion). Malachite alleviates shyness and supports
friendships. The stone strengthens the ability to process
information, helping to understand difficult concepts.
Malachite is a soul-cleanser. It attunes to angelic and
spiritual guidance, and has a strong affinity with nature.
The stone facilitates scrying, or inner or outer journeying,
as it enhances intuition and insight.

Vibration: Earthy and high
Chakra: Earth star, Gaia gateway, base, sacral, heart, solar plexus
Physiology: Joints, muscles, optic nerve, DNA, cellular
structure, immune system, liver, pain receptors
Cleansing: All

CHRYSOPRASE
Divine wholeness

Chrysoprase helps you to feel part of the divine whole. It promotes hope and offers personal insights. Encouraging fidelity in business and personal relationships, it draws out talents and stimulates creativity, bringing openness to new situations. Healing codependence, Chrysoprase supports independence while encouraging commitment. It reviews egotistical motives and the effect on personal development, aligning ideals with behaviour. Overcoming compulsive or impulsive thoughts and actions, it turns attention to positive events. Chrysoprase opposes judgementalism, stimulating acceptance of your Self and others. It assists forgiveness and compassion. It averts nightmares, especially among children.

Vibration: Earthy
Chakra: Sacral
Physiology: Infertility, eyes, skin, heart, thyroid, hormonal balance, digestive system
Cleansing: Avoid water

CHRYSOCOLLA
Heartfelt communication

Facilitating verbal expression, Chrysocolla empowers
both sexes to communicate in a clear, loving way. Gentle
Chrysocolla transmutes negative energy, healing scars
on the emotional body. It alleviates guilt and brings joy,
easing judgementalism, especially of your own Self, and
encourages compassion to all. Chrysocolla helps you to
love yourself—vital if you are to accept love from others.
An aid to meditation, it opens psychic vision and accepts
with serenity changing situations, especially those over
which you have no control. It encourages self-awareness
and inner balance, invoking inner strength to speak
your truth.

Vibration: Earthy
Chakra: Sacral, solar plexus, heart, throat, third eye
Physiology: Metabolism, pancreas, thyroid, throat, female
reproductive system, digestive tract, liver, kidneys, intestines,
bones, blood
Cleansing: Avoid water, unless tumbled

Crystals
for the mind

Over-thinking, too much mind-chatter, closed-mindedness, limiting beliefs and mental control by others all lead to dis-ease—as does the strong, but largely unrecognized, effect on the mind of emotions such as excessive worry and shame. Fortunately, crystals quickly switch off the chattering mind, clarifying thought and embracing the dynamic mindfulness of the present moment, rather than obsessively worrying about past or future. They enhance mental function at all levels, reprogramming thought patterns where appropriate, assisting memory and bringing brain hemispheres back into balance.

Thought Forms

Thought forms may appear to be solid and "real" and yet have no actual substance. But they have a profound effect on how you function mentally. Typical thought forms are the critic, the saboteur and the perfectionist. Created by powerfully negative or controlling mental input, thought forms may be the product of your own mind or arise from other people's expectations or authoritarian dictates. They lodge themselves in the mental subtle body as an internal thought form or lurk in the ancestral or past-life subtle bodies. Internal thought forms are usually experienced as a derogatory inner voice or obsessive thoughts. They emanate subtle feelings of disapproval or command. External thought forms inhabit the lower astral realms close to Earth, and may speak as an inner voice, although often appearing as separate entities such as guides or metaphysical communicators.

HOW TO RECOGNIZE AND CLEAR A THOUGHT FORM

- A nagging voice gives negative messages such as "that's a bad thing to do," "you're not good enough," "it's all your fault," "you'll never be/get what you want," "you don't deserve," or "you're too clever for your own good."
- It feels subtly wrong.
- It may resemble someone you know, especially if they have passed on.
- It has little substance or resonance to it.
- The "guidance" is fallible and may be malicious.
- It seems to be stuck in a loop.

To remove an external thought form, dedicate a large thought-form dissolving crystal such as Iolite and leave it in a room to do its work. Internal thought forms tend to be stored in the third-eye chakra or just behind the ears. Use a Selenite wand to detach them or place a thought-form dissolving crystal over the site. Aegerine is excellent for mental obsession if you can't get someone or something out of your mind. Place it under the pillow at night. Remember to cleanse the crystal frequently.

Addiction

Addiction takes two forms. The physical, in which the body becomes biologically dependent on a substance or act, and the psychological, in which the mind compulsively uses a substance or action to quell underlying stress, emotions such as shame or a sense of inferiority, or traumatic memories. Crystals assist in breaking the cycle of dependency, facilitating stress release and instant mindfulness. Mindfulness means being aware in the moment, focused on the present, not somewhere back in the past or projected into the future. It's not mindlessness, which acts by rote, or meditation, but rather a dynamic yet soft attentiveness. It's about living each moment in your daily life to the full, and then flowing onto the next.

EXERCISE
TAKING TIME OUT

Crystal mindfulness takes only a few moments, but makes an enormous difference to your life.

Suitable crystals: Anything banded, such as Banded Agate; or calming, such as Amethyst, Auralite 23, Amazez, Eye of the Storm, Selenite.

- Keep a suitable calming crystal in your pocket.
- Every so often, especially when stressed, take it out, hold it close to your eyes and focus on it until it fills your mind.
- Breathe deeply and slowly ten times, making the out-breath longer than the in-breath.
- Return the crystal to your pocket.

AMETHYST
Addiction-breaker

Amethyst heals subtle dis-ease. Stilling the mind, it takes it to a mindful space. An excellent stress reliever, Amethyst enhances memory and decision-making and improves motivation. Relieving the compulsions, obsessions and neediness that underlie addictions, it dispels anger, fear, rage and anxiety and comforts grief. Protective Amethyst guards against psychic attack, enhances higher states of consciousness and facilitates meditation and spiritual awareness. Repelling negative energies of all kinds, it screens out EMF smog or geopathic stress.

Vibration: High to extremely high
Chakra: All, depending on type
Physiology: All, depending on type, cells, hormonal and immune system, intestines
Cleansing: All

SNOWFLAKE OBSIDIAN
Emergence

Snowflake Obsidian gently surfaces toxic emotions, detrimental thought patterns and traumatic memories. Revealing destructive life patterns, it reframes them in a more beneficial way. It also surfaces unexpectedly positive secrets. This serene stone provides balance during times of stress and change, and shields against negativity. In past-life work, Snowflake Obsidian heals ingrained karmic patterns and reveals sources of harmful thought patterns. It teaches you to be receptive and value mistakes as well as successes, showing the gift in each. Snowflake Obsidian turns loneliness into at-oneness.

Vibration: Earthy
Chakra: Base, sacral
Physiology: Veins, skeleton, circulation, skin, eyes, joints
Cleansing: All

GREEN AVENTURINE
Spleen protector

Green Aventurine protects the spleen chakra. Circling it under the left armpit removes hooks from past relationships and detaches energy vampires who drain your energy. The stone prevents reattachment. It protects and heals the heart. Ameliorating fear, it examines motives and outdated behaviour patterns, dissolving negative emotions and thoughts. Green Aventurine looks forward with joyous expectation and provides support if you are going outside your comfort zone. It increases confidence and brings out leadership qualities, strengthening integrity and compassion. The stone has strong links with increasing fertility. It enhances your own creativity.

Vibration: Earthy
Chakra: Base, sacral, heart, spleen
Physiology: Spleen, eyes, kidneys, adrenals, lungs, sinuses, heart, muscular system, blood pressure
Cleansing: All

GREEN CALCITE
Mental cleanser

Dissolving rigid beliefs and outdated mental programming, Green Calcite restores balance and clarity to the mind. It lets go of the familiar and comforting that are outgrown and which no longer serve. The stone facilitates communication on all levels and helps children to hold their own in debates. A powerful stimulator for the immune system, it rapidly absorbs negativity and rids the body of bacterial infections. Green Calcite soothes nausea, pain and inflammation. It increases fertility and attracts abundance—drawing prosperity into a home. It is useful in grids, but cleanse it frequently.

Vibration: Earthy to high
Chakra: Solar plexus, spleen
Physiology: Stomach
Cleansing: All

FLUORITE
Organizer

Excellent for processing information so that the mind becomes sharper, Fluorite overcomes any disorganization or stress, physical or mental. It improves coordination and counteracts mental disorders. No matter which colour, this stone dissolves fixed ideas and illusions and reveals the truth behind a situation. Helpful when you need to act objectively, it gives you inner strength and stability to withstand internal or external influences and pressure. Fluorite cleanses and stabilizes the aura, grounding and integrating spiritual energies. It heightens intuitive powers and enhances trance states.

Vibration: Medium to high
Chakra: Heart, higher heart, third eye
Physiology: Brain, joints, bones, teeth, muscles and acts as an anti-inflammatory
Cleansing: Avoid water

LAPIS LAZULI
Heaven on earth

Lapis Lazuli is a powerful stress releaser. It encourages self-expression and taking charge of your own life, facilitating self-awareness so that you see the bigger picture. Lapis Lazuli brings objectivity and clarity to the mind and teaches the value of active listening. A stone of deep spiritual insight, it stimulates psychic abilities and clairvoyance, and facilitates spiritual journeying to contact spirit guardians and mentors. The stone blocks psychic attack. Placing it on psychic or past-life chakras reverses curses and clears dis-ease caused by not speaking out in the past.

Vibration: Extremely high
Chakra: Throat, third eye, crown
Physiology: Immune system, respiratory and nervous systems, throat, larynx, thyroid, ears, internal organs, bone marrow, blood
Cleansing: All

CITRINE
Abundance characteristics

Prized for its prosperity-enhancing properties, Citrine encourages generosity of spirit and accumulation of wealth. It reminds you that abundance is a state of mind that encompasses friendship and joy as well as money. The bright energy of Citrine counts your blessings and raises your self-confidence. Excellent for counteracting depression, this crystal instils optimism and a positive attitude. It overcomes apathy and hopelessness, and raises self-esteem. A stone of creativity, Citrine capitalizes on your skills and talents. Stimulating your mind, it facilitates seeing new possibilities and actualizing them. Despite Citrine being largely self-cleansing, it benefits from regular clearing.

Vibration: Extremely high
Chakra: Sacral, crown
Physiology: Digestion, kidneys, blood, thymus, thyroid, hormonal and immune systems
Cleansing: All

BLUE TOPAZ
Writer's friend

Excellent for written communication and expressing yourself more fully, Blue Topaz enhances mental abilities, encouraging clear thought and focused concentration. Helpful for public speaking, it clears the throat and third-eye chakras. If you need to make decisions about matters in your life, such as the ideal job or how to implement your lifepath, meditate with Blue Topaz. It connects to the angels of truth and wisdom, facilitating living according to your own aspirations and recognizing whether you have strayed from your truth. If so, Blue Topaz gently assists you to let go of limiting beliefs embracing spiritual independence.

Vibration: High
Chakra: Third eye, throat
Physiology: Eyes, throat
Cleansing: All

SODALITE
Mental integration

Healing a disordered mind, restoring normal functioning of intuitive perception and encouraging rational thought, Sodalite facilitates reception and integration of new information. It releases control mechanisms that are holding you back from being who you truly are, enhancing self-esteem, self-acceptance and self-trust. Uniting logic with intuition, it opens spiritual inner-sight, bringing information from the higher mind to the physical level. It stimulates the third eye and deepens meditative states. Sodalite relieves the symptoms of dyslexia and dyspraxia. Bringing emotional balance, it calms panic attacks. The stone creates harmony in group work.

Vibration: High
Chakra: Throat, third eye
Physiology: Metabolism, lymphatic system, internal organs, immune system, throat, digestive system
Cleansing: All

BLUE CHALCEDONY
Speaker's aid

Opening the mind to assimilate new ideas, Blue Chalcedony stimulates learning new languages. It improves memory, encouraging mental flexibility and enhancing verbal dexterity and listening skills. Measuring your words before you speak, it facilitates holding back what you may later regret. The stone encourages reflection and imparts the ability to look forward optimistically, facilitating acceptance of change and improving self-perception. Excellent for clearing illnesses associated with weather and pressure changes, it wards off psychic attack and protects during political unrest. Useful for the eyes, it promotes inner-sight and insight.

Vibration: High
Chakra: Throat, third eye
Physiology: Mucous membranes, eyes, immune and lymphatic systems, blood pressure
Cleansing: All

AMETRINE
Spiritual clarity

Connecting the physical realm with higher consciousness, Ametrine stimulates creativity and supports taking control of life. It imbues mental clarity, harmonizing perception and action and resolving apparent contradictions. Protecting against stress and creating inner well-being, Ametrine heightens concentration. It facilitates thinking things through, encouraging exploration of all possibilities. Enhancing acceptance of others, it overcomes prejudice. Protective during journeying, Ametrine guards against psychic attack. It brings insight into underlying causes of emotional distress, raising deep-seated issues to the surface. Its powerful cleansing properties disperse negativity from the aura and toxins from the body.

Vibration: High
Chakra: All
Physiology: Blood, metabolism, immune and autonomic nervous systems, DNA/RNA, oxygenation
Cleansing: All

Crystals for the spirit

Holding divine light and unity consciousness, crystals have a natural affinity with the realm of soul, spirit and Higher Self. Ideal for soul-healing and connecting to the soulplan for the present lifetime, they create the perfect mode of communication at metaphysical levels, opening expanded awareness and higher consciousness and linking it deep into Mother Earth.

EXERCISE

TO OPEN THE INNER EYE

When the higher crown chakras are connected to the earth chakras, it grounds your inner sight, located in the third eye, which is facilitated by the use of crystals.

- Place a grounding stone such as Flint, Hematite, Shungite or Smoky Quartz at your feet.
- With your eyes closed, look up to your inner screen, between and slightly above your eyebrows.
- Place a third-eye crystal such as Apophyllite or Labradorite mid-forehead.
- Absorb the crystal energy so that it opens your third eye.
- If there is resistance or a headache develops, replace the crystal with Rhomboid Selenite or Bytownite, pulling energy down into your belly and to the crystal at your feet until the blockage clears.

CONTACTING THE HIGHER SELF

A vehicle for soul consciousness, the Higher Self's vibration is less dense than that of the physical body, extending beyond the purely physical realm and therefore seeing much further. Crystals assist in raising your physical vibrations sufficiently for your Higher Self to manifest on the earth-plane. A simple visualization makes contact.

Suitable crystals: Selenite, Anandalite, Kyanite, Bytownite or other Higher Self crystals.

- Settle yourself comfortably, placing a grounding stone at your feet, such as Flint, Hematite, or Smoky Quartz.
- Take a big breath and sigh out any tension you may be feeling.
- Hold your crystal over the heart seed chakra. Feel the chakra opening like the petals of a flower, connecting the heart and higher heart and opening the three-chambered heart chakra.

- Take your crystal up to the crown chakra. Feel the chakra opening. The higher crown chakras above your head expand and a string-like sensation pulls you up as you take the crystal to the highest point you can reach. Allow your vibrations to rise.
- Invite your Higher Self to move down through the higher crown chakras until it fills your crown chakra. From the crown chakra, it moves into the three-chambered heart.
- Experience the love that your Higher Self has for you, drawing that love deep into your being. Welcome it, learning to trust and feeling safe.
- When you are ready to end the exercise, ask your Higher Self to remain connected to your heart.
- Close the chakras above your head, folding them in like flowers closing for the night. Close the crown and third eye chakras.
- Leave the three-chambered heart open, making sure that your earth star chakra is holding you firmly in incarnation—that is, in your physical body and not floating a foot off the planet.
- Slowly bring your attention back to your physical body and the room around you.

EXERCISE

INTEGRATING SOUL AND PSYCHE

The figure of eight or lemniscate layout integrates "above" with "below" and facilitates profound soul-healing. The layout draws spiritual energy down into the body and melds it with earth-energy drawn up from the feet to create perfect balance and core energy solidity.

- Place high-vibration stones from the waist to above the crown and down again.
- Place grounding stones from the waist to below the feet and up again.
- To complete the grid, place an integration stone at the crossover point.
- Complete the circuit back to the first stone.

LABRADORITE
Interface

Placed on the third-eye or past-life chakras, Labradorite clears psychic debris from previous disappointments and removes other people's projections and expectations.

This highly mystical crystal is a bringer of light, containing esoteric knowledge. Raising consciousness and connecting with universal energies, it takes you into another world or other lives.

Deflecting unwanted energies from the energy bodies and preventing energy leakage, it is excellent for screening yourself while allowing awareness of what is happening in another field. This crystal opens intuition and activates psychic gifts. Labradorite banishes fears and insecurities. It strengthens trust in your Self and the universe.

Vibration: High
Chakra: Higher heart, throat, third eye; aligns all
Physiology: Brain, eyes, metabolic and hormonal systems
Cleansing: Avoid water

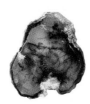

MERLINITE
Magical

Merlinite holds the combined knowledge of shamans, alchemists, magician-priests and workers of magic to support spiritual evolution. It blends spiritual and earthly vibrations, accessing multidimensional shamanic realms. Helpful if you are undergoing the dark night of the soul, Merlinite brings harmony into the present life, balancing yin–yang, masculine and feminine energies, conscious and subconscious, intellect and intuition.

Vibration: Extremely high
Chakra: Third eye
Physiology: Heart, nervous, respiratory and circulatory systems, intestines, heart, karmic blueprint
Cleansing: All

ANGEL AURA QUARTZ
Angelic guidance

Serene Angel Aura Quartz is created by fusing platinum, silver or gold onto Quartz to create a highly supportive spiritual energy of exquisite purity. The iridescence shines like the wings of angels—hence the name—and contacts guardian angels and angelic guidance. This crystal facilitates remembering soul lessons from past incarnations and attuning to present-life soul purpose. It clears the throat chakra and encourages loving communication. Angel Aura aligns all chakras and harmonizes subtle bodies with the physical. It can soothe anxiety, panic attacks and phobias.

Vibration: High
Chakra: Throat
Physiology: Nervous system
Cleansing: Avoid water or abrasives

MOLDAVITE
Time traveller

Moldavite fuses extraterrestrial energies with Mother Earth, taking you way beyond your limits and bringing you into contact with your Higher Self and star beings. Moldavite integrates the divine blueprint and accelerates spiritual growth. It assimilates information so that you become fully conscious. Detaching from security issues such as money and worries for the future, it takes you forward to see the results of actions taken in the present, or to learn what is needed now to create a positive future.

Vibration: Extremely high
Chakra: Third eye, higher crown
Physiology: Etheric bodies
Cleansing: Avoid water and earth

TURQUOISE
Protector

Promoting spiritual attunement and facilitating communication with angelic realms, protective Turquoise enhances intuition and meditation. It explores past lives and shows without judgement how the creation of seeming "fate" is an ongoing response to previous actions that were neither "good" nor "bad." They simply were. This strengthening stone is excellent for exhaustion, depression or panic attacks. It calms nerves when speaking in public, dissolves self-sabotage, facilitates creative expression and stabilizes mood swings. Turquoise is anti-inflammatory, benefiting gout, rheumatism, cramps, arthritis and similar dis-eases. A pain reliever, it protects against airborne pollutants and allergies.

Vibration: High
Chakra: Throat, third eye
Physiology: Immune system
Cleansing: All

AQUAMARINE
Courage

Aquamarine reduces fear or stress and removes extraneous
thoughts, filtering information reaching the brain
and clarifying perception. It dissolves self-defeating
programmes, allowing the soul to be heard. Having an
affinity with sensitive people, Aquamarine invokes tolerance
of others. Overcoming judgementalism, it supports
those overwhelmed by responsibility, and encourages
responsibility for your Self. Counteracting the forces of
darkness and procuring favour from the Spirits of Light—
angels and higher beings—it brings unfinished business to
a conclusion and ensures closure on all levels. Aquamarine
clears blocked communication and assists self-expression
and understanding underlying emotional states.

Vibration: High
Chakra: Throat, third eye; aligns all
Physiology: Throat, glands, thyroid, pituitary, hormonal system,
cleansing organs, eyes, jaw, teeth, stomach, immune and auto-
immune systems
Cleansing: All

BLUE KYANITE
Ultimate healing

Amplifying high-frequency energies, Blue Kyanite aligns chakras and subtle bodies, clearing pathways and meridians. It encourages speaking your highest truth, cutting through fears, illusions and blockages and increasing capacity for logical thought. Kyanite is tranquillizing, inducing deep meditative states, and yet stimulates psychic abilities. Facilitating detaching from the idea of blind fate or implacable karma, Blue Kyanite reveals measures required to balance out the past. Grounding and mediating the flow of spiritual energy, Kyanite restores Qi to the physical body and is a natural pain reliever. It restabilizes the energy bodies and soul after transformation.

Vibration: Extremely high
Chakra: Throat, third eye, crown
Physiology: Muscles, temperature control, thyroid, adrenal glands, throat, brain
Cleansing: Avoid water

ANGELITE
Angelic connection

Deepening attunement and heightening spiritual perception, Angelite facilitates angelic contact. It enhances telepathic communication and out-of-body journeys. Angelite opens psychic channelling from the highest sources, connecting to universal knowledge and raising awareness of multidimensional realms. It facilitates speaking your truth and being more compassionate, accepting that which cannot be changed. Preventing psychic overwhelm, Angelite creates a protective auric shield and balances etheric and physical energies. A useful stress and tension reliever, it overcomes fear and anger and fosters forgiveness.

Vibration: High
Chakra: Throat, third eye, crown
Physiology: Thyroid, meridians, soft tissue, blood vessels, fluid balance
Cleansing: All

CELESTITE
Reintegrating the soul

Celestite assists angelic communication and remembers the divine nature of your soul. Connecting to your guardian angel, it stimulates clairvoyance and promotes dream recall and out-of-body journeys. Supporting your spiritual development at the highest level, this crystal teaches trust in the infinite wisdom of the universe. It facilitates conflict resolution and instils balance in times of stress. Carry one if you are a "worrywart." Celestite's gentle vibes cool fiery emotions and the crystal quietens and sharpens the mind, promoting mental clarity and fluent communication.

Vibration: High
Chakra: Throat, third eye, crown
Physiology: Eyes, ears, throat, muscles, elimination systems
Cleansing: All

APOPHYLLITE
Third-eye activator

Creating a conscious connection between physical and spiritual realms, Apophyllite accesses multidimensions. This metaphysical stone opens the third eye, particularly if this was blocked in previous lives, stimulating intuition and clairvoyance. Facilitating journeys into past lives and enhancing telepathy and channelling, the crystal promotes introspection into your own behaviour, highlighting the part you played in what was created and the consequences. It brings about recognition of one's true Self. A stress reducer, Apophyllite releases suppressed emotions and overcomes anxiety, worries and fears. It neutralizes allergies and has been found to assist during asthma attacks.

Vibration: High
Chakra: Heart, third eye, crown
Physiology: Eyes, mucous membranes, skin, respiratory system
Cleansing: Avoid water

SELENITE
Crystallized divine light

Inhabiting the space between light and matter, translucent Selenite anchors the lightbody into the Earth vibration, and downloads divine light into the physical body. It creates a safe, peaceful space that does not allow outside influences to penetrate. Selenite detaches entities from the aura and prevents anything external from influencing the mind. It reaches into other lives, or the future, and checks progress made with the current lifeplan, pinpointing lessons and issues being worked upon. Bringing about a conscious understanding of what is occurring at the subconscious level, it shows how it can best be resolved.

Vibration: Extremely fine
Chakra: Crown
Physiology: Spinal column, teeth, bones
Cleansing: Avoid water

Judy Hall was an internationally known author, astrologer, crystal expert, psychic and healer. A leading authority on spiritual development, Judy had more than 45 years of experience in karmic astrology, crystal healing and past-life therapy. She was the author of over 45 books— including the bestselling *The Crystal Bible*, which has sold more than 1 million copies worldwide. Judy was four times named as one of the 100 most spiritually influential people in the world in the Watkins Review.